SALLY WISTER'S JOURNAL

A True Narrative

BEING A QUAKER MAIDEN'S ACCOUNT
OF HER EXPERIENCES WITH OFFICERS
OF THE CONTINENTAL ARMY, 1777-1778

APPLEWOOD BOOKS
BEDFORD, MASSACHUSETTS

Sally Wister's Journal was originally published in 1902.

ISBN 1–55709–114–5

Thank you for purchasing an Applewood Book.
Applewood reprints America's lively classics—books from
the past that are of interest to modern readers.
For a free copy of our current catalog, write to:
Applewood Books, Box 365, Bedford, MA 01730.

6 8 10 9 7 5

Library of Congress Cataloging-in-Publication Data:
Wister, Sarah, 1761–1804.
[Journal]
Sally Wister's journal: a true narrative: being a
Quaker maiden's account of her experiences
with officers of the Continental Army, 1777–1778.
p.   cm.
Originally published in 1902.
ISBN 1–55709–114–5
1. Pennsylvania—History—Revolution, 1775–1783—
Personal narratives.   1. United States—History—
Revolution, 1775–1783—Personal narratives.
3. Wister, Sarah, 1761–1804—Diaries.   I. Title
E263.P4W8   1995
973.3'8–dc20
94–43038
CIP

SALLY WISTER'S JOURNAL

To Deborah Norris:—

Tho' I have not the least shadow of an opportunity
to send a letter, if I do write, I will keep a sort of journal of the time that may expire before I see thee: the
perusal of it may some time hence give pleasure in a
solitary hour to thee and our Sally Jones.

Yesterday, which was the 24th of September, two
Virginia officers call'd at our house, and inform'd us that
the British Army has cross'd the Schuylkill. Presently
after, another person stopp'd, and confirm'd what they
had said, and that Gen'l Washington and Army were
near Pottsgrove. Well, thee may be sure we were sufficiently scared; however, the road was very still till
evening.

About seven o'clock we heard a great noise. To the
door we all went. A large number of waggons, with
about three hundred of the Philadelphia Militia. They
begged for drink, and several push'd into the house.
One of those that entered was a little tipsy, and had a
mind to be saucy.

I then thought it time for me to retreat; so figure me (mightily scar'd, as not having presence of mind enough to face so many of the Military), running in at one door, and out another, all in a shake with fear; but after a while, seeing the officers appear gentlemanly, and the soldiers civil, I call'd reason to my aid. My fears were in some measure dispell'd tho' my teeth rattled, and my hand shook like an aspen leaf. They did not offer to take their quarters with us; so, with many blessings, and as many adieus, they marched off.

I have given thee the most material occurrences of yesterday faithfully.

Fourth Day, September 25th.

This day, till twelve o'clock, the road was mighty quiet, when Hobson Jones came riding along. About that time he made a stop at our door, and said the British were at Skippack road; that we should soon see their light horse, and [that] a party of Hessians had actually turn'd into our lane. My Dadda and Mamma gave it the credit it deserv'd, for he does not keep strictly to the truth in all respects; but the delicate, chicken-hearted Liddy and I were wretchedly scar'd. We cou'd say nothing but "Oh! what shall we do? What will become of us?" These questions only augmented the terror we were in.

Well, the fright went off. We saw no light horse or Hessians. O. Foulke came here in the evening, and told us that Gen'l Washington had come down as far as the Trappe, and that Gen'l McDougle's brigade was stationed at Montgomery, consisting of about 16 hundred men. This he had from Dr. Edwards, Lord Stirling's aid-de-camp; so we expected to be in the midst of one army or t'other.

Fourth Day Night.

We were not alarm'd.

Fifth Day, September 26th.

We were unusually silent all the morning; no passengers came by the house, except to the Mill, & we don't place much dependence on Mill news.

About twelve o'clock, cousin Jesse heard that Gen. Howe's army had moved down towards Philadelphia. Then, my dear, our hopes & fears were engaged for you. However, my advice is, summon up all your resolution, call Fortitude to your aid, and don't suffer your spirits to sink, my dear; there's nothing like courage; 'tis what I stand in need of myself, but unfortunately have little of it in my composition.

I was standing in the kitchen about 12, when somebody came to me in a hurry, screaming, "Sally, Sally, here are the light horse!" This was by far the greatest fright I had endured; fear tack'd wings to my feet; I was at the house in a moment; at the porch I stopt, and it really was the light horse.

I ran immediately to the western door, where the family were assembled, anxiously waiting for the event. They rode up to the door and halted, and enquired if we had horses to sell; he was answer'd negatively.

"Have not you, sir," to my father, "two black horses?"

"Yes, but have no mind to dispose of them."

My terror had by this time nearly subsided. The officer and men behav'd perfectly civil; the first drank two glasses of wine, rode away, bidding his men follow, which, after adieus in number, they did. The officer was Lieutenant Lindsay, of Bland's regiment, Lee's troop. The men, to our great joy, were Americans, and but 4 in all. What made us imagine them British, they wore blue and red, which with us is not common.

It has rained all this afternoon, and to present appearances, will all night. In all probability the English will take possession of the city to-morrow or next day. What a change will it be! May the Almighty take you under His protection, for without His divine aid all human assistance is vain.

> "May heaven's guardian arm protect my absent friends,
> From danger guard them, and from want defend."

Forgive my dear, the repetition of these lines, but they just darted into my mind.

Nothing worth relating has occurred this after-noon. Now for trifles. I have set a stocking on the needles, and intend to be mighty industrious. This evening

some of our folks heard a very heavy cannon. We sup-
posed it to be fir'd by the English. The report seem'd to
come from Philad^a. We hear the American army will be
within five miles of us tonight.

The uncertainty of our position engrosses me quite.
Perhaps to be in the midst of war, and ruin, and the
clang of arms. But we must hope the best.

Here, my dear, passes an interval of several weeks,
in which nothing happen'd worth the time and paper
it wou'd take to write it. The English, however, in the
interim, had taken possession of the city.

Second Day, October the 19th, 1777.

Now for new and uncommon scenes. As I was lying
in bed, and ruminating on past and present events, and
thinking how happy I shou'd be if I cou'd see you,
Liddy came running into the room, and said there was
the greatest drumming, fifing, and rattling of waggons
that ever she had heard. What to make of this we were
at a loss. We dress'd and down stairs in a hurry. Our
wonder ceas'd.

The British had left Germantown, and our Army
was marching to take possession. It was the general
opinion that they wou'd evacuate the capital. Sister
Betsy and myself, and G. E. went about half a mile
from home, where we cou'd see the army pass. Thee
will stare at my going, but no impropriety in my opine,

or I wou'd not have gone. We made no great stay, but return'd with excellent appetites for our breakfast.

Several officers call'd to get some refreshment, but none of consequence till the afternoon. Cousin Prissa and myself were sitting at the door; I in a green skirt, dark short gown, &c. Two genteel men of the military order rode up to the door: "Your servant, ladies," &c; ask'd if they cou'd have quarters for Genl. Smallwood. Aunt Foulke thought she cou'd accommodate them as well as most of her neighbours,—said they could. One of the officers dismounted, and wrote

> SMALLWOOD'S QUARTERS

over the door, which secured us from straggling soldiers. After this he mounted his steed and rode away.

When we were alone our dress and lips were put in order for conquest, and the hopes of adventures gave brightness to each before passive countenance.

Thee must be told of a Dr. Gould, who, by accident, had made and acquaintance with my father,—a sensible, conversible man, a Carolinian,—and had come to bid us adieu on his going to that state. Daddy had prevailed upon him to stay a day or two with us.

In the evening his Generalship came with six attendants, which compos'd his family, a large guard of soldiers, a number of horses and baggage-waggons. The yard and house were in confusion, and glitter'd with military equipments.

Gould was intimate with Smallwood, and had gone into Jesse's to see him. While he was there, there was great running up and down stairs, so I had an opportunity of seeing and being seen, the former the most agreeable, to be sure. One person, in particular, attracted my notice. He appear'd cross and reserv'd; but thee shall see how agreeably disappointed I was.

Dr. Gould usher'd the gentlemen into our parlour, and introduced them,—"Gen'l Smallwood, Capt. Furnival, Major Stodard, Mr. Prig, Capt. Finley, and Mr. Clagan, Col. Wood, and Col. Line." These last two did not come with the Gen'l. They are Virginians, and both indispos'd. The Gen'l and suite are Marylanders.

Be assur'd I did not stay long with so many men, but secur'd a good retreat, heart-safe, so far. Some sup'd with us, others at Jesse's. They retir'd about ten, in good order.

How new is our situation! I feel in good spirits, though surrounded by an Army, the house full of officers, the yard alive with soldiers,—very peaceable sort of men, tho'. They eat like other folks, talk like them, and behave themselves with elegance; so I will not be afraid of them, that I won't.

Adieu. I am going to my chamber to dream, I suppose, of bayonets and swords, sashes, guns, and epaulets.

Third Day Morn., October 20th.

I dare say thee is impatient to know my sentiments of the officers; so, while Somnus embraces
them, and the house is still, take their characters
according to their rank.

The General is tall, portly, well made: a truly martial air, the behaviour and manner of a gentleman, a
good understanding, & great humanity of disposition,
constitute the character of Smallwood.

Col. Wood, from what we hear of him and what
we see, is one of the most amiable of men; tall and genteel, an agreeable countenance and deportment. These
following lines will more fully characterize him:

> "How skill'd he is in each obliging art,
> The mildest manners with the bravest heart."

The cause he is fighting for alone tears him from the
society of an amiable wife and engaging daughter; with
tears in his eyes he often mentions the sweets of domes-
tic life.

Col. Line is not married; so let me not be too
warm in his praise, lest you suspect. He is monstrous
tall & brown, but has a certain something in his face
and conversation very agreeable; he entertains the
highest notions of honour, is sensible and humane, and
a brave officer; he is only seven and twenty years old,
but, by a long indisposition and constant fatigue, looks
vastly older, and almost worn to a skeleton, but very

lively and talkative.

Capt. Furnival,—I need not say more of him than that he has, excepting one or two, the handsomest face I ever saw, a very fine person; fine light hair and a great deal of it, adds to the beauty of his face.

Well, here comes the glory, the Major, so bashful, so famous, &c. He shou'd come before the Captain, but never mind. I at first thought the Major cross and proud, but I was mistaken. He is about nineteen, nephew to the Gen'l, and acts as Major of brigade to him; he cannot be extoll'd for the graces of person, but for those of the mind he may justly be celebrated; he is large in his person, manly, and an engaging countenance and address.

Finley is wretched ugly, but he went away last night, so shall not particularize him.

Nothing of any moment to-day; no acquaintance with the officers. Col. Wood and Line and Gould din'd with us. I was dressed in my chintz, and look'd smarter than night before.

Fourth-Day, Oct. 21st.

I just now met the Major, very reserv'd; nothing but "Good morning," or "Your servant, madam"; but Furnival is most agreeable; he chats every opportunity; but luckily has a wife!

I have heard strange things of the Major. Worth a fortune of thirty thousand pounds, independent of anybody; the Major, moreover, is vastly bashful; so much so he can hardly look at the ladies. (Excuse me, good sir; I really thought you were not clever; if 'tis bashfulness only, we will drive that away.)

Fifth-day, Sixth-day, and Seventh-day pass'd. The Gen'l still here; the Major still bashful.

First-Day Evening.

Prepare to hear amazing things. The Gen'l was invited to dine, was engag'd; but Col. Wood and Line, Maj^r Stodard, and Dr. Edwards din'd with us.

In the afternoon, Stodard, addressing himself to mamma, "Pray, ma'am, do you know Miss Nancy Bond?" I told him of the amiable girl's death. This major had been to Philad^a College.

In the evening, I was diverting Johnny at the table, when he drew his chair to it, and began to play with the child. I ask'd him if he knew N. Bond. "No, ma'am, but I have seen her very often." One word brought on another, and we chatted the greatest part of the evening. He said he knew me directly when he saw me. Told me exactly where we liv'd. It rains now, so adieu.

Second-Day, 26th October.

A very rainy morning, so like to prove. The officers in the house all day.

Second-Day Afternoon.

The General and officers drank tea with us, and stay'd part of the evening. After supper I went into aunt's where sat the Gen'l, Col. Line, and Major Stodard. So Liddy and I seated ourselves at the table in order to read a verse-book.

The Major was holding a candle for the Gen'l, who was reading a newspaper. He look'd at us, turn'd away his eyes, look'd again, put the candlestick down, up he jump'd, out of the door he went.

"Well," said I to Liddy, "he will join us when he comes in."

Presently he return'd, and seated himself on the table.

"Pray, ladies, is there any songs in that book?"

"Yes, many."

"Can't you fav^r me with a sight of it?"

"No, Major, 'tis a borrow'd book."

"Miss Sally, can't you sing?"

"No."

Thee may be sure I told the truth there. Liddy, saucy girl, told him I cou'd. He beg'd and I deny'd; for my voice is not much better than the voice of a raven. We talk'd and laugh'd for an hour. He is very clever, amiable, and polite. He has the softest voice, never pronounces the R at all.

I must tell thee, to-day arriv'd Col. Guest and

Major Letherberry; the former a smart widower, the latter a lawyer, a sensible young fellow, and will never swing for want of tongue.

Dr. Diggs came Second-day; a mighty disagreeable man. We were oblig'd to ask him to tea. He must needs prop himself between the Major and me, for which I did not thank him. After I had drank tea, I jump'd from the table, and seated myself at the fire. The M—— followed my example, drew his chair close to mine, and entertain'd me very agreeably.

Oh, Debby; I have a thousand things to tell thee. I shall give thee so droll an account of my adventures that thee will smile. "No occasion of that, Sally," methinks I hear thee say, "for thee tells me every trifle." But, child, thee is mistaken, for I have not told thee half the civil things that are said of us *sweet* creatures at "General Smallwood's Quarters." I think I might have sent the gentlemen to their chambers. I made my adieus, and home I went.

Third Day Morn.

A polite "Good morning" from the M——, more sociable than ever. No wonder; a stoic cou'd not resist such affable damsels as we are.

Third Day Eve., October 27th.

We had again the pleasure of the Gen'l and suite at afternoon tea. He (the Gen'l, I mean) is most agreeable; so lively, so free, and chats so gaily, that I have quite an esteem for him. I must steel my heart! Capt. Furnival is gone to Baltimore, the residence of his belov'd wife.

The Major and I had a little chat to ourselves this eve. No harm, I assure thee: he and I are friends.

This eve came a parson belonging to the Army. He is (how shall I describe him?) near seven foot high, thin and meagre, not a single personal charm, and very few mental ones. He fell violently in love with Liddy at first sight; the first discover'd conquest that has been made since the arrival of the Gen'l.

Come, shall we chat about Col. Guest? He's very pretty; a charming person; his eyes are exceptional; very stern; and he so rolls them about that mine always fall under them. He bears the character of a brave officer; another admirer of Liddy's, and she is of him.

When will Sally's admirers appear? Ah! that indeed. Why, Sally has not charms sufficient to pierce the heart of a soldier. But still I won't despair. Who knows what mischief I yet may do?

Well, Debby, here's Dr. Edwards come again. Now we shall not want clack; for he has a perpetual motion in his head, and if he was not so clever as he is, we shou'd get tired.

Fourth Day, October 28th.

Nothing material engag'd us to-day.

Fifth Day, October 29th.

I walk'd into aunt's this evening. I met the Major. Well, thee will think I am writing his history; but not so. Pleased with the rencounter, Liddy, Betsy, Stodard, and myself, seated by the fire, chatted away an hour in lively and agreeable conversation. I can't pretend to write all he said; but he shone in every subject that we talk'd of.

Sixth Day Eve, October 30th.

Nothing of consequence.

Seventh Day, October 31st.

A most charming day. I walk'd to the door and received the salutation of the morn from Stodard and other officers. As often as I go to the door, so often have I seen the Major. We chat passingly, as, "A fine day, Miss Sally." "Yes, very fine, Major."

Seventh Day Night.

Another very charming conversation with the young Marylander. He seem'd possessed of very amiable manners; sensible and agreeable. He has by his unexceptionable deportment engag'd my esteem.

First Day Morn.

Liddy, Betsy, and a T. L., prisoner of this State, went to the Mill. We made very free with some

Continental flour. We powder'd mighty white, to be sure. Home we came.

Col. Wood was standing at a window with a young officer. He gave him a push forward, as much as to say, "Observe what fine girls we have here." For all I do not mention Wood as often as he deserves, it is not that we are not sociable: we are very much so, and he is often at our house, dines or drinks tea with us every day.

Liddy and I had a kind of an adventure with him this morn. We were in his chamber, chatting about our little affairs, and no idea of being interrupted: we were standing up, each an arm on a chest of drawers; the door bang'd open!—Col. Wood was in the room; we started, the colour flew into our faces and crimson'd us over; the tears flew into my eyes. It was very silly; but his coming was so abrupt. He was between us and the door.

"Ladies, do not be scar'd, I only want something from my portmanteau; I beg you not to be disturbed."

We ran by him like two partridges, into mamma's room, threw ourselves into chairs, and reproach'd each other for being so foolish as to blush and look so silly. I was very much vex'd at myself, so was Liddy. The Col. laugh'd at us, and it blew over.

The Army had orders to march to-day; the regulars accordingly did. Gen'l Smallwood had the command of Militia at that time, and they being in the rear, were not to leave their encampment until Second-day.

Observe how militaryish I talk. No wonder, when I am surrounded by people of that order.

The Gen'l, Colonels Wood, Line, Guest, Crawford, Majors Stodard and Letherberry, din'd with us to-day. After dinner Liddy, Betsy, and thy smart journalizer, put on their bonnets determined to take a walk.

We left the house. I naturally look'd back; when, behold, the two majors seem'd debating whether to follow us or not. Liddy said, "We shall have their attenddance", but I did not think so. They open'd the gate, and came fast after us. They overtook us about ten pole from home, and beg'd leave to attend us. No fear of a refusal.

They enquir'd where we were going. "To neighbour Roberts's. We will introduce you to his daughters; you us to Gen'l Stevens."

The affair was concluded, and we shortened the way with lively conversation.

Our intention of going to Roberts's was frustrated; the rain that had fall'n lately had rais'd Wissahickon too high to attempt crossing it on foot. We alter'd the plan of our ramble, left the road, and walk'd near two miles thro' the woods.

M. Letherberry, observing my locket, repeated with the energy of a comedian—

> "On her white neck a sparkling cross she wore,
> That Jews might kiss or infidels adore."

I repli'd my trinket bore no resemblance to a cross.

"'Tis something better, ma'am."

'Tis nonsense to pretend to recount all that was said; my memory is not so obliging; but it is sufficient that nothing happen'd during our little excursion but what was very agreeable and entirely consistent with the strictest rules of politeness & decorum.

I was vex'd a little at tearing my muslin petticoat. I had on my white whim, quite as nice as a First-day in town. We returned home safe.

Smallwood, Wood, and Stodard drank tea with us, and spent the greatest part of the evening.

I declare this Genl is very, very entertaining, so good natur'd, so good humour'd, yet so sensible; I wonder he is not married. Are there no ladies form'd to his taste?

Some people, my dear, think that there's no difference between good nature and good humour; but, according to my opinion, they differ widely. Good nature consists in a naturally amiable and even disposition, free from all peevishness and fretting. It is accompanied by a natural gracefulness,—a manner of doing and saying everything agreeably; in short, it steals the senses and captivates the heart. Good humour consists in being pleas'd, and who wou'd thank a person for being cheerful, if they had nothing to make them otherways. Good humour is a very agreeable companion for an afternoon; but give me good nature for life.

Adieu.

Second Day Morn, November 1st.

To-day the Militia marches, and the Gen'l and officers leave us. Heigh ho! I am very sorry; for when you have been with agreeable people, 'tis impossible not to feel regret when they bid you adieu, perhaps forever. When they leave us we shall be immur'd in solitude.

The Major looks dull.

Second Day Noon.

About two o'clock the Gen. and Major came to bid us adieu. With daddy and mammy they shook hands very friendly; to us they bow'd politely.

Our hearts were full. I thought Major was affected.

"Good-bye, Miss Sally," spoken very low. He walk'd hastily and mounted his horse. They promised to visit us soon.

We stood at the door to take a last look, all of us very sober.

The Major turn'd his horse's head, and rode back, dismounted.

"I have forgot my pistols," pass'd us, and ran upstairs.

He came swiftly back to us, as if wishing, through inclination, to stay; by duty compell'd to go. He remounted his horse.

"Farewell, ladies, till I see you again," and canter'd away.

We look'd at him till the turn in the road hid him

from our sight. "Amiable major," "Clever fellow," "Good young man," was echo'd from one to the other. I wonder whether we shall ever see him again. He has our wishes for his safety.

Well, here's Uncle Miles. Heartily glad of that am I. His family are well, and at Reading.

Second Day Even.

Jesse, who went with the Gen'l, return'd. I had by him a letter from my dear Polly Fishbourn. She is at George Emlen's. Headquarters is at their house. We had compliments from the Gen'l and Major. They are very well disposed of at Evan Meredith's, six miles from here. I wrote to Polly by Uncle Miles, who waited upon Gen'l Washington next morn.

Third Day Morn, November 2d.

It seems strange not to see our house as it used to be. We are very still. No rattling of waggons, glittering of musquets. The beating of the distant drum is all we hear.

Cols. Wood, Line, Guest and M. Letherberry are still here; the two last leave us to-day. Wood and Line will soon bid us adieu. Amiable Wood; he is esteem'd by all that know him! Everybody has a good word for him.

Here I skip a week or two, nothing of consequence

occurring. Wood & Line are gone. Some time since arriv'd two officers, Lieutenant Lee and Warring, Virginians. I had only the salutations of the morn from them.

Lee is not remarkable one way or the other; Warring an insignificant piece enough. Lee sings prettily, and talks a great deal; how good turkey hash and fry'd hominy is—(a pretty discourse to entertain the ladies),—extols Virginia and execrates Maryland, which, by-the-by, I provok'd them to; for though I admire both Virg^a and Mary^d, I laugh'd at the former and prais'd the latter. Ridiculed their manner of speaking. I took great delight in teasing them. I believe I did it sometimes ill-natur'dly; but I don't care. They were not, I am certain almost, first-rate gentlemen. (How different from our other officers.) But they are gone to Virginia, where they may sing, dance, and eat turkey hash and fry'd hominy all day long, if they choose.

Nothing scarcely lowers a man in my opinion more than talking of eating, what they love and what they hate. Lee and Warring were proficients in this science. Enough of them!

December 5th, Sixth Day.

Oh, gracious! Debby, I am all alive with fear. The English have come out to attack (as we imagine) our army. They are on Chestnut Hill, our army three miles this side. What will become of us, only six miles distant?

We are in hourly expectation of an engagement. I fear we shall be in the midst of it. Heaven defend us from so dreadful a sight. The battle of Germantown, and the horrors of that day, are recent in my mind. It will be sufficiently dreadful if we are only in hearing of the firing, to think how many of our fellow-creatures are plung'd into the boundless ocean of eternity, few of them prepar'd to meet their fate. But they are summon'd before an all-merciful Judge, from whom they have a great deal to hope.

Seventh Day, December 6th.

No firing this morn. I hope for one more quiet day.

Seventh Day; 4 o'clock.

I was much alarm'd just now, sitting in the parlour, indulging melancholy reflections, when somebody burst open the door, "Sally, here's Major Stodard!"

I jumped. Our conjectures were various concerning his coming. The poor fellow, from great fatigue and want of rest, together with being expos'd to the night air, had caught cold, which brought on a fever. He cou'd scarcely walk, and I went into aunt's to see him.

I was surpris'd. Instead of the lively, alert, blooming Stodard, who was on his feet the instant we enter'd, he look'd pale, thin, and dejected, too weak to rise. A bow, and "How are you, Miss Sally?"

"How does thee do, Major?"

I seated myself near him, inquir'd the cause of his indisposition, ask'd for the Gen'l, receiv'd his compliments. Not willing to fatigue him with too much chat, I bid him adieu.

To-night Aunt Hanna Foulke, Senr, administer'd something. Jesse assisted him to his chamber. He had not lain down five minutes before he was fast asleep. Adieu. I hope we shall enjoy a good night's rest.

First Day Morn, December 7th.

I trip'd into aunt's. There sat the Major, rather more like himself. How natural it was to see him.

"Good morning, Miss Sally."

"Good morrow, Major, how does thee do to-day?"

Major: "I feel quite recover'd."

Sally: "Well, I fancy this indisposition has sav'd thy head this time."

Major: "No, ma'am; for if I hear a firing, I shall soon be with them." That was heroic.

About eleven, I dress'd myself, silk and cotton gown. It is made without an apron. I feel quite awkwardish, and prefer the girlish dress.

First Day Afternoon

A Mr. Seaton and Stodard drank tea with us. He and I had a little private chat after tea.

In the eve, Seaton went into aunt's; mamma went to see Prissa, who is poorly; papa withdrew to talk to some strangers. Liddy just then came in, so we engag'd in an agreeable conversation.

I beg'd him to come and give us a circumstantial account of the battle, if there should be one.

"I certainly will, ma'am, if I am favor'd with life."

Liddy, unluckily, took it into her head to blunder out something about a person being in the kitchen who had come from the army.

Stodard, ever anxious to hear, jump'd up. "Good night to you, Ladies," was the word, and he disappeared, but not forever.

"Liddy, thee hussy; what business had thee to mention a word of the army? Thee sees it sent him off. Thy evil genius prevail'd, and we all feel the effects of it."

"Lord bless me," said Liddy, "I had not a thought of his going, or for ten thousand worlds I wou'd not have spoke." But we cannot recall the past.

Well, we laugh'd and chatted at a noisy rate, till a summons for Liddy parted us. I sat negligently on my chair, and thought brought on thought, and I got so low spirited that I cou'd hardly speak. The dread of an engagement, the dreadful situation (if a battle shou'd ensue) we should be in, join'd to my anxiety for P. Fishbourn and family, who would be in the midst of the scene, was the occasion.

And yet I did not feel half so frighten'd as I expected to be. 'Tis amazing how we get reconciled to such things. Six months ago the bare idea of being within ten, aye twenty miles, of a battle, wou'd almost have distracted me. And now, tho' two such large armies are within six miles of us, we can be cheerful and converse calmly of it. It verifies the old proverb, that "Use is second nature."

I forgot one little piece of intelligence, in which the girls say I discover'd a particular partiality for our Marylanders, but I disclaim anything of the kind. These saucy creatures are forever finding out wonders, and forever metamorphosing mole-hills into mountains.

> "Friendship I offer, pure and free;
> And who, with such a friend as ME,
>   Could ask or wish for more?"

"If they charg'd thee with vanity, Sally, it wou'd not be very unjust." Debby Norris! be quiet; no reflections, or I have done. "But the piece of intelligence, Sally!" [It] is just coming, Debby.

In the afternoon we distinctly heard platoon firing. Everybody was at the door; I in the horrors. The armies, as we judg'd, were engag'd.

Very compos'dly says the Major to our servant, "Will you be kind enough to saddle my horse? I shall go!"

Accordingly, the horse was taken from the hospitable quiet barn to plunge into the thickest ranks of war. Cruel change!

Seaton insisted to the Major that the armies were

still; "nothing but skirmishing with the flanking parties; do not go."

We happen'd (we girls, I mean) to be standing in the kitchen, the Maj. passing thro' in a hurry, and I, forsooth, discover'd a strong partiality by saying, "Oh! Major, thee is not going!"

He turn'd around, "Yes, I am, Miss Sally," bow'd, and went into the road; we all pitied him.

The firing rather decreas'd; and after persuasions innumerable from my father and Seaton, and the firing over, he reluctantly agreed to stay. Ill as he was, he would have gone. It show'd his bravery, of which we all believe him possess'd of a large share.

Second Day, December 8th.

Rejoice with us, my dear. The British have return'd to the city. Charming news this. May we ever be thankful to the Almighty Disposer of events for his care and protection of us while surrounded with dangers.

Major went to the army. Nothing for him to do; so returned.

Third- or Fourth-day, I forget which, he was very ill; kept his chamber most of the day. In the evening I saw him. He has a violent sore mouth. I pity him mightily, but pity is a poor remedy.

Fifth Day, December 11th.

Our Army mov'd, as we thought, to go into winter

quarters, but we hear there is a party of the enemy gone over Schuylkill; so our Army went to look at them.

I observ'd to Stodard, "So you are going to leave us to the English."

"Yes, ha! ha! ha! leave you for the English."

He has a certain indifference about him sometimes that to strangers is not very pleasing. He sometimes is silent for minutes. One of these silent fits was interrupted the other day by his clasping his hands and exclaiming aloud, "Oh, my God, I wish this war was at an end!"

Noon.

The Major gone to camp. I don't think we shall see him again.

Well, strange creature that I am; here have I been going on without giving thee an account of two officers,—one who will be a principal character; their names are Capt. Lipscomb and a Mr. Tilly; the former a tall, genteel man, very delicate from indisposition, and has a softness in his countenance that is very pleasing, and has the finest head of hair that I ever saw; 'tis a light, shining auburn. The fashion of his hair was this—negligently ty'd and waving down his back. Well may it be said,—

"Loose flow'd the soft redundance of his hair."

He has not hitherto shown himself a lady's man,

tho' he is perfectly polite.

Now let me attempt to characterize Tilly. He seems a wild, noisy mortal, tho' I am not much acquainted with him. He appears bashful when with girls. We dissipated the Major's bashfulness; but I doubt we have not so good a subject now. He is above the common size, rather genteel, an extreme pretty, ruddy face, hair brown, and a sufficiency of it, a very great laughter, and talks so excessively fast that he often begins sentences without finishing the last, which confuses him very much, and then he blushes and laughs; and in short, he keeps me in perpetual good humour; but the creature has not address'd one civil thing to me since he came.

But I have not done with his accomplishments yet, for he is a musician,—that is, he plays on the German flute, and has it here.

Fifth Day Night.

The family retir'd; take the adventures of the afternoon as they occurr'd.

Seaton and Capt. Lipscomb drank tea with us. While we sat at tea, the parlour door was open'd; in came Tilly; his appearance was elegant; he had been riding; the wind had given the most beautiful glow to his cheeks, and blow'd his hair carelessly round his face.

Oh, my heart, thought I, be secure!

The caution was needless, I found it without a wish to stray.

When the tea equipage was remov'd, the conversation turned on politicks, a subject I avoid. I gave Betsy a hint. I rose, she followed, and went to seek Liddy.

We chatted a few moments at the door. The moon shone with uncommon splendour. Our spirits were high. I propos'd a walk; the girls agreed. When we reached the poplar tree, we stopp'd. Our ears were assail'd by a number of voices.

"A party of light horse," said one.

"The English, perhaps; let's run home."

"No, no," said I, "be heroines."

At last two or three men on horseback came in sight. We walked on. The well-known voice of the Major saluted our hearing with, "How do you do, ladies?"

We turn'd ourselves about with one accord. He, not relishing the idea of sleeping on the banks of the Schuylkill, had return'd to the Mill.

We chatted along the road till we reach'd our hospitable mansion. Stodard dismounted, and went into Jesse's parlour. I sat there a half hour. He is very amiable.

Seaton, Lipscomb, Tilly, and my father, hearing of his return, and impatient for the news, came in at the door, while I made my exit at the other.

I am vex'd at Tilly, who has his flute, and does nothing but play the fool. He begins a tune, plays a note or so, then stops. Well, after a while, he begins again;

stops again. "Will that do, Seaton? Hah! hah! hah!"

He has given us but two regular tunes since he arriv'd. I am passionately fond of music. How boyish he behaves.

Sixth day, December 12th, 1777.

I ran into aunt's this morn to chat with the girls. Major Stodard join'd us in a few minutes.

I verily believe the man is fond of the ladies, and, what to me is astonishing, he has not discovered the smallest degree of pride. Whether he is artful enough to conceal it under the veil of humility, or whether he has none, is a question; but I am inclined to think it the latter.

I really am of opinion that there are few of the young fellows of the modern age exempt from vanity, more especially those who are bless'd with exterior graces. If they have a fine pair of eyes they are ever rolling them about; a fine set of teeth, mind, they are great laughers; a genteel person, forever changing their attitudes to show them to advantage. Oh, vanity, vanity; how boundless is thy sway!

But to resume this interview with Major Stodard. We were very witty and sprightly. I was darning an apron, upon which he was pleas'd to compliment me.

"Well, Miss Sally, what would you do if the British were to come here?"

"Do," exclaimed I; "be frightened just to death."

He laugh'd, and said he would escape their rage by getting behind the representation of a British grenadier which you have upstairs. "Of all things, I should like to frighten Tilly with it. Pray, ladies, let's fix it in his chamber to-night."

"If thee will take all the blame, we will assist thee."

"That I will," he replied, and this was the plan.

We had brought some weeks ago a British grenadier from Uncle Miles's on purpose to divert us. It is remarkably well executed, six foot high, and makes a martial appearance. This we agreed to stand at the door that opens into the road (the house has four rooms on a floor, with a wide entry running through), with another figure that would add to the deceit. One of our servants was to stand behind them, others were to serve as the occasion offer'd.

After half an hour's converse, in which we rais'd our expectations to the highest pitch, we parted. If our scheme answers, I shall communicate in the eve. Till then, adieu. 'Tis dining hour.

Sixth Day Night.

Never did I more sincerely wish to possess a descriptive genius than I do now. All that I can write will fall infinitely short of the truly diverting scene that I have been witness to to-night. But, as I mean to attempt an account, I had as well shorten the preface, and begin the story.

In the beginning of the eveng I went to Liddy and beg'd her to secure the swords and pistols which were in their parlour. The Marylander, hearing our voices, joined us. I told him of my proposal. Whether he thought it a good one or not I can't say, but he approv'd of it, and Liddy went in and brought her apron full of swords & pistols.

When this was done, Stodard join'd the officers. We girls went and stood at the first landing of the stairs. The gentlemen were very merry and chatting on public affairs, when Seaton's negro (observe that Seaton, being indisposed, was appriz'd of the scheme) open'd the door, candle in his hand, and said, "There's somebody at the door that wishes to see you."

"Who? All of us?" said Tilly.

"Yes, sir," answer'd the boy.

They all rose (the Major, as he afterwards said, almost dying with laughing), and walk'd in to the entry, Tilly first, in full expectation of news.

The first object that struck his view was a British soldier. In a moment his ears were saluted, "Is there any rebel officers here?" in a thundering voice.

Not waiting for a second word, he darted like lightning out at the front door, through the yard, bolted o'er the fence. Swamps, fences, thorn-hedges, and plough'd fields no way impeded his retreat. He was soon out of hearing.

The woods echoed with, "Which way did he go? Stop him! Surround the house!" The amiable Lipscomb had his hand on the latch of the door, intending to attempt his escape; Stodard, considering his indisposition, acquainted him with the deceit.

We females ran down stairs to join in the general laugh. I walked into Jesse's parlour. There sat poor Stodard (whose sore lips must have receiv'd no advantage from this), almost convuls'd with laughing, rolling in an arm-chair. He said nothing; I believe he could not have spoke.

"Major Stodard," said I, "go call Tilly back. He will lose himself,—indeed he will;" every word interrupted with a "Ha! ha!"

At last he rose, and went to the door, and what a loud voice could avail in bringing him back, he tried.

Figure to thyself this Tilly, of a snowy eveng, no hat, shoes down at heel, hair unty'd, flying across meadows, creeks and mud-holes. Flying from what? Why, a bit of painted wood. But he was ignorant of what it was. The idea of being made a prisoner wholly engross'd his mind, and his last resource was to run.

After a while, we being in rather more composure, and our bursts of laughter less frequent, yet by no means subsided,—in full assembly of girls and officers,— Tilly enter'd.

The greatest part of my risibility turn'd to pity. Inexpressible confusion had taken entire possession of his countenance, his fine hair hanging dishevell'd down his shoulders, all splashed with mud; yet his fright, confusion and race had not divested him of his beauty.

He smil'd as he trip'd up the steps; but 'twas vexation plac'd it on his features. Joy at that moment was banished from his heart. He briskly walked five or six steps, then stopt, and took a general survey of us all.

"Where have you been, Mr. Tilly?" ask'd one officer. (We girls were silent.)

"I really imagin'd," said Stodard, "that you were gone for your pistols. I follow'd you to prevent danger,"—an excessive laugh at each question, which it was impossible to restrain.

"Pray, where were your pistols, Tilly?"

He broke his silence by the following expression: "You may all go to the D——l." I never heard him utter an indecent expression before.

At last his good natured gain'd a complete ascendance over his anger, and he join'd heartily in the laugh. I will do him the justice to say that he bore it charmingly. No cowardly threats, no vengeance denounced.

Stodard caught hold of his coat. "Come, look at what you ran from," and drag'd him to the door.

He gave it a look, said it was very natural, and, by the singularity of his expressions, gave fresh cause for diversion. We all retir'd to our different parlours, for to rest our faces, if I may say so.

Well, certainly, these military folks will laugh all night. Such screaming I never did hear. Adieu tonight.

Seventh-day Morn, December 13th.

I am fearful they will yet carry the joke too far. Tilly certainly possesses an uncommon share of good nature, or he could not tolerate these frequent teasings.

Ah, Deborah, the Major is going to leave us entirely—just going. I will see him first.

Seventh Day Noon.

He has gone. I saw him pass the bridge. The woods, which you enter immediately after crossing it, hinder'd us from following him farther. I seem to fancy he will return in the eveng.

Seventh Day Night.

Stodard not come back. We shall not, I fancy, see him again for months, perhaps years, unless he should visit Philadᵃ. We shall miss his agreeable company.

But what shall we make of Tilly? No civil things yet from him. Adieu to-night, my dear.

First Day Morn, December, 14th.

The officers yet here. No talk of their departure. They are very lively. Tilly's retreat the occasion; the principal one, however [at least].

First Day Night.

Capt. Lipscomb, Seaton, and Tilly, with cousin
Hannah Miles, din'd with us to-day. Hannah's health
seems establish'd, to our great joy.

Such an everlasting laugher as Tilly I never knew.
He caus'd us a good deal of diversion while we sat at
table. He has not said a syllable to one of us young
ladies since Sixth-day eve. He tells Lipscomb that the
Major had the assistance of the ladies in the execution
of the scheme. He tells a truth.

About four o'clock I was standing at the door, lean-
ing my head on my hand, when a genteel officer rode
up to the gate and dismounted. "Your servant, ma'am,"
and gave me the compliment of his hat. Walk'd into
aunt's.

I went into our parlour. Soon Seaton was call'd.
Many minutes had not elapsed before he entered with
the same young fellow whom I had just seen. He introduced him by the name of Capt. Smallwood. We seated ourselves. I then had an opportunity of seeing him.

He is a brother to Gen'l Smallwood. A very genteel, pretty little fellow, very modest, and seems agreeable, but no personal resemblance between him and the
Major.

After tea, turning to Tilly, he said,

"So, sir, I have heard you had like to have been made
a prisoner last Friday night!"

"Pray, sir, who informed you?"

"Major Stodard was my author."

"I fancy he made a fine tale of it. How far did he say I ran?"

"Two mile; and that you fell into the mill-dam!"

He rais'd his eyes and hands, and exclaimed, "What a confounded falsehood!"

The whole affair was again reviv'd.

Our Tillian Hero gave a mighty droll account of his retreat, as they call it. He told us that after he had got behind our kitchen he stop'd for company, as he expect-ed the others wou'd immediately follow. "But I heard them scream, 'Which way did he go? Where is he?' 'Aye,' said I, to myself, 'he is gone where you shan't catch him,' and off I set again."

"Pray," ask'd mamma, "did thee keep that lane between the meadows?"

"Oh, no, ma'am; that was a large road, and I might happen to meet some of them. When I reach'd yon thorn hedge, I again stop'd. As it was a cold night, I thought I would pull up my shoe heels, and tye my handkerchief round my head. I then began to have a suspicion of a trick, and, hearing the Major hollow, I came back."

I think I did not laugh more at the very time than to-night at the rehearsal of it. He is so good-natured, and takes all their jokes with so good a grace, that I am quite charm'd with him. He laughingly denounces vengeance against Stodard. He will be even with him.

He is in the Major's debt, but he will pay him.

Second-day Eveng, December 15th.

Smallwood has taken up his quarters with us. Nothing worth relating occur'd to-day.

3d, 4th and Fifth-day.

We chatted a little with the officers. Smallwood not so chatty as his brother or nephew. Lipscomb is very agreeable; a delightful musical voice.

Sixth-day Noon, Dec. 19th.

The officers, after the politest adieus, have left us. Smallwood and Tilly are going to Maryland, where they live; Seaton to Virginia; and Lipscomb to Camp, to join his regiment. I feel sorry at their departure, yet 'tis a different kind from what I felt some time since. We had not contracted so great an intimacy with those last.

Seventh-day, December 20th.

General Washington's army have gone into winter quarters at the Valley Forge.

We shall not see many of the military now. We shall be very intimate with solitude. I am afraid stupidity will be a frequent guest.

After so much company, I can't relish the idea of sequestration.

First-day Night.

A dull round of the same thing over again. I shall
hang up my pen till something offers worth relating.

February Third or Fourth, I for[get which?]

I thought I shou'd never have anything to say again.
Nothing happen'd all January that was uncommon.
Capt. Lipscomb and Mos (?) stay'd one night at Jesse's;
sup'd with us. How elegant the former was dress'd and
how pretty he look'd.

Indeed I have forgot to keep an exact account of the
day of the month in which I went down to George
Emlen's with P. Fishbourn, but it was the 23d or 24th
of February (?). After enjoying a week of her agreeable
company at the Mill, I returned with her to
Whitemarsh. We went on horseback, the roads bad.
We however surmounted this difficulty, and arrived
there safe.

Frd. Fishbourn and P. Talman were there. It gave
me great pleasure to see people whom I esteem after so
very long an absence. We spent an agreeable afternoon.
In the eveng Frd. F. and P. T. return'd to their home
about a mile or two distant.

Second-day Eve.

G. E. brought us a charming collection of books,—
"Joe Andrews," "Juliet Grenville," and some *Lady's*

Magazines. P. T. sent us "Caroline Melmoth."

Third-day, February 25th.

Rose between eight and nine, breakfasted, read & worked by turns, chatted agreeably. I think Sally Emlen is one of the most beautiful women I ever saw, agreeable, affable, sensible in the true sense of the words. Her conversation is so very lively and diverting that were her personal attractions less than they are she cou'd not fail of being belov'd. She has one lovely daughter.

Third-day Even.

This day Mrs. and Miss West visited here. I did not feel in a humour capable of entertaining or being entertain'd, so I sat very still. Spent the eve in reading and chatting of the past, present and future.

We talk of going to frd. Fishbourn's to-morrow.

Fourth-day, 26th.

I thought this morn that our scheme of going to Fr'd F. was entirely frustrated, as S. Emlen was much indispos'd with the headache. About twelve she got better. We made some alterations in our dress, step'd into the carriage, and rode off. Spent a most delightful day.

As we approach'd the house, on our return, we perceiv'd several strangers in the parlour. Polly's face and mine brighten'd up at the discovery. We alighted. Polly swung open the door, and introduc'd me to Major Jameson & Capt. Howard, both of the dragoons, the former of Virginia, the latter a Marylander.

We all seem'd in the penseroso style till after supper. We then began to be rather more sociable. About ten they bid us adieu.

I dare say thee is impatient to know my sentiments of the swains. Howard has very few external charms; indeed, I cannot name one. As to his internal ones, I am not a judge. Jameson is tall and manly, a comely face, dark eyes and hair. Seems to be much of a gentleman. No ways deficient in point of sense, or, at least, in the course of the eveng, I discover'd none.

Fifth- and Sixth-day, and 7th-day pass'd away very agreeably. No strangers.

First-day Eve.

This morn my charming friend and self ascended the barren hills of Whitemarsh, from the tops of which we had an extensive prospect of the country round. The traces of the Army which encamp'd on these hills are very visible,—ragged huts, imitations of chimneys, and many other ruinous objects, which plainly show'd they had been there. D. J. Shoemaker dined with us.

Second Day.

Very cold and windy. I wonder I am not sent for. Read and work'd by turns.

Third Day.

A raw, snowy day. I am sent for, nevertheless. Adieu.

North Wales, at my old habitation at the Mill.
March 1st, 1778, Third Day Eve.

Such a ride as I have had, O dear Debby(?). About 2 o'clock the sleigh came for me. Snowing excessively fast, though not sufficiently deep to make it tolerable sleighing; but go I must. I bid adieu to my agreeable frds, and with a heavy heart & flowing eyes, I seated myself in the unsociable vehicle.

There might as well have been no snow on the ground. I was jolted just to pieces. But, notwithstanding these vexations, I got safe to my home, when I had the great pleasure of finding my dear parents, sisters and brother well, a blessing which I hope ever to remember with thankfulness.

Well, will our nunnery be more bearable now than before I left it? No beaus since I left here, so I have the advantage of the girls. They are wild to see Major Jameson.

May 11th, 1778.

The scarcity of paper, which is very great in this part of the country, and the three last months producing hardly anything material, has prevented me from keeping a regular account of things; but to-day the scene begins to brighten, and I will continue my non-sense.

In the afternoon, we were just seated at tea,—Dr. Moore with us. Nelly (our girl) brought us the wonderful intelligence that there were light horse in the road. The tea-table was almost deserted. About 15 light horse were the vanguard of 16 hundred men under the command of Gen'l Maxwell. I imagin'd that they wou'd pass immediately by, but I was agreeably disappointed. My father came in with the Gen'l, Col. Broadhead, Major Ogden and Capt. Jones. The Gen'l is a Scotsman,—nothing prepossessing in his appearance; the Col¹ very martial and fierce; Ogden, a genteel young fellow, with an aquiline nose.

Captain Cadwallader Jones—if I was not invincible, I must have fallen a victim to this man's elegancies, but (thank my good fortune, I am not made of susceptibilities),—tall, elegant and handsome,—white fac'd, with blue regimentals, and a mighty airish cap and white crest; his behaviour is refin'd—a Virginian. They sat a few minutes after tea, then bid us adieu.

This brigade is encamp'd about three miles from us.

First Day Evening.

This afternoon has been productive of adventures in the true sense of the word. Jenny Roberts, Betsy, Liddy, and I, very genteelly dress'd, determined to take a stroll. Neighbor Morgan's was proposed and agreed to.

Away we rambled, heedless girls. Pass'd two picket guards. Meeting with no interruptions encourag'd us.

After paying our visit, we walked towards home, when, to my utter astonishment, the sentry desir'd us to stop; that he had orders not to suffer any persons to pass but those who had leave from the officer, who was at the guard house, surrounded by a number of men. To go to him would be inconsistent with propriety; to stay there, and night advancing, was not clever.

I was much terrified. I try'd to persuade the soldier to let us pass. "No; he dared not." Betsy attempted to go. He presented his gun, with the bayonet fix'd. This was an additional fright.

Back we turn'd; and, very fortunately, the officer, Capt. Emeson [Emerson], seeing our distress, came to us. I ask'd him if he had any objection to our passing the sentry. "None at all, ma'am." He waited upon us, and reprimanded the man, and we, without any farther difficulty, came home.

Third Day, June 2d, 1778.

I was standing at the back window. An officer and private of dragoons rode by. I tore to the door to have a better view of them. They stopped. The officer rode up, and ask'd for Jesse, who was call'd.

Third-day Afternoon, 4 o'clock.

Oh, Deborah; what capital adventures. Jesse came.

The idea of having light horse quarter'd at the farm was disagreeable; the meadows just fit to mow, and we had heard what destruction awaited their footsteps.

This was the dialogue between Jesse and the officer:

"Pray, sir, can I have quarters for a few horsemen?"

"How many."

"Five and twenty, sir. I do not mean to turn them into your meadows. If you have any place you can spare, anything will do."

And he dismounted, and walk'd into aunt's parlour. I, determined to find out his character, follow'd.

"I have," reply'd Jesse, "a tolerable field, that perhaps may suit."

"That will do, sir. But if you have any objection to putting them in a field, my men shall cut the grass, and bring it in the road. I am under the necessity of quartering them here, but I was order'd. I am only an inferior officer."

Some elegant corporal, thought I, and went to the door. He soon join'd me, speaking to his man, "Ride off, and tell Mr. Watts we rendezvous here."

He inquir'd the name of the farmer, and went to aunt's; I into the back room. The troop rode up. "New scenes," said I, and mov'd upstairs, where I saw them perform their different manœuvres.

This Mr. Watts is remarkably tall, and a good countenance. I adjourn'd to our parlour. This first officer march'd up and down the entry. Prissa came in.

"Good, now, Prissa. What's the name of this man?"

"Dyer, I believe. Capt. Dyer." Oh, the name!

"What does he say?"

"Why, that he will kiss me when he has din'd."
"Singular," I observ'd, "on so short an acquaintance."

"But," resum'd Prissa, "he came and fix'd his arm on the chair I sat in:

"Pray, ma'am, is there not a family from town with you?'

"'Yes.'

"'What's their name?'

"'Wister.'

"'There's two fine girls there. I will go chat with them. Pray, did they leave their effects in Philad^a?'

"'Yes, everything, almost.'

"'They shall have them again, that they shall.'"

There ended the conversation. But this ugly name teas'd me.

"Oh, Sally, he is a Virginian; that's in his fav^r greatly. I'm not sure that's his name, but I understood so."

Prissa left us. I step'd into aunt's for Johnny and desir'd him to come home. Up started the Captain:

"Pray, let me introduce you, ma'am."

"I am perfectly acquainted with him," said I, and turned to the door.

"Tell your sister I believe she is not fond of strangers."

I smil'd, and returned to our parlour.

Third Day Night, nine o'clock, aye ten, I fancy.

Take a circumstantial account of this afternoon, and the person of this extraordinary man. His exterior first. His name is not Dyer, but Alexander Spotswood Dandridge, which certainly gives a genteel idea of the man. But I will be particular.

His person is more elegantly form'd than any I ever saw; tall and commanding. His forehead is very white, tho' the lower part of his face is much sunburn'd; his features are extremely pleasing; an even, white set of teeth, dark hair and eyes. I can't better describe him than by saying he is the handsomest man I ever beheld. Betsy and Liddy coincide in this opinion.

After I had sat a while at home, in came Dandridge. He enter'd into chat immediately. Ask'd if we knew Tacy Vanderen. Said he courted her, and that they were to be married soon. Observ'd my sampler, which was in full view, Wish'd I would teach the Virginians some of my needle wisdom; they were the laziest girls in the world. Told his name. Laugh'd and talk'd incessantly.

At last, "May I" (to mamma) "introduce my brother officer?" We assented; so he call'd him.

"Mr. Watts, Mrs. Wister, young Miss Wisters. Mr. Watts, ladies, is one of our Virginia children."

He sat down. Tea was order'd. Dandridge never drank tea. Watts had done; so we sat to the tea-table alone.

"Let's walk in the garden," said the Captain; we cal-l'd Liddy, and went (not Watts). We sat down in a sort of a summer-house.

"Miss Sally, are you a Quaker?"

"Yes."

"Now, are you a Quaker?"

"Yes, I am."

"Then you are a Tory."

"I am not, indeed."

"Oh, dear," reply'd he, "I am a poor creature. I can hardly live."

Then, flying away from that subject,

"Will you marry me, Miss Sally?"

"No, really; a gentleman after he has said he has not sufficient to maintain himself, to ask me to marry him."

"Never mind what I say, I have enough to make the pot boil."

Had we been acquainted seven years, we could not have been more sociable. The moon gave a sadly pleas-ing light. We sat at the door till nine.

Dandridge is sensible (and divest'd of some free-doms, which might be call'd gallant in the fashionable world), he is polite and agreeable. His greatest fault is a propensity to swearing, which throws a shade over his accomplishments. I ask'd him why he did so. "It is a favorite vice, Miss Sally." At nine he went to his chamber. Sets off at sunrise.

Fourth Day Morn, 1 2 o'clock.

I was awaken'd at four this morn with a great racket
of the Captain's servant calling him; but the lazy fellow
never rose till about half an hour before eight. This his
daylight ride.

I imagin'd they would be gone before now, so I
dressed in a green'h skirt and dark short gown.
Provoking. So down I came, this Captain (wild
wretch) standing at the back door. He bow'd and call'd
me. I only look'd, and went to breakfast.

About nine I took my work and seated myself in the
parlour. Not long had I sat, when in came
Dandridge,—the handsomest man in existence, at least
that I have ever seen.

But stop here, while I just say, the night before,
chatting upon dress, he said he had no patience with
those officers who, every morn, before they went on
detachments, wou'd wait to be dress'd and powder'd.

"I am," said I, "excessively fond of powder, and
think it very becoming."

"Are you?" he reply'd. "I am very careless, as often
wearing my cap thus" (turning the back part before) "as
any way."

I left off where he came in. He was powder'd very
white, a (pretty colour'd) brown coat, lapell'd with
green, and white waistcoat, &c., and his

"Sword beside him negligently hung."

He made a truly elegant figure.

"Good morning, Miss Sally. You are very well, I hope."

"Very well. Pray sit down," which he did, close by me. "Oh, dear," said I, "I see thee is powder'd."

"Yes, ma'am. I have dress'd myself off for you."

Will I be excused, Debby, if I look upon his being powder'd in the light of a compliment to me? "Yes, Sally, as thee is a country maid, and don't often meet with compliments." Saucy Debby Norris!

'Tis impossible to write a regular account of our conversation. Be it sufficient to say that we had a multiplicity of chat.

About an hour since, sister Hannah came to me and said Captain Dandridge was in the parlour, and had asked for me. I went in. He met me, caught my hands. "Oh, Miss Sally, I have a beautiful sweetheart for you."

"Poh! ridiculous! Loose my hands."

"Well, but don't be so cross."

"Who is he!"

"Major Clough."

"I have seen him. Ain't he pretty, to be sure?"

"I am going to headquarters. Have you any commands there?"

"None at all; but (recollecting), yes, I have. Pray, who is your commanding officer?"

"Col. Bland, ma'am."

"Please give my compliments to him, and I shou'd be glad if he wou'd send thee back with a little more manners."

He reply'd wickedly, and told me I had a little spiteful heart. But he was intolerably saucy; said he never met with such ladies.

"Not to let me kiss you. You're very ill-natured, Miss Sally."

And putting on the sauciest, sober face, "Sally, if Tacy V-nd-r-n won't have me, will you?"

"No, really; none of her discarded lovers."

"But, provided I prefer you to her, will you consent?"

"No, I won't."

"Very well, madam."

And, after saying he would return to-morrow, among a hundred other things, he elegantly walk'd out of the room.

Soon he came back, took up a volume of Homer's Iliad, and read to us. He reads very well, and with judgment. One remark he made, that I will relate, on these lines,—

> "While Greece a heavy, thick retreat maintains,
>   Wedg'd in one body, like a flight of cranes."

"God knows our Army don't do so. I wish they did."

He laugh'd, threw down the book, left his sword, and went away.

Four o'clock, Afternoon.

Major Clough, Captain Swan, and Mr. Moore, a lieutenant of horse, din'd with Dandridge. The latter, after dinner, came in to bid us adieu. He sat down, and was rather saucy. I look'd very grave.

"Miss Betsy, you have a very ill-natur'd sister. Observe how cross she looks."

He prayed we might part friends, and offer'd his hand. I gave him mine, which he kiss'd in a very gallant manner; and so, with a truly affectionate leave, he walk'd to the parlour door, "God Almighty bless you, ladies;" bow'd, went into the road, mounted a very fine horse, and rode away; leaving Watts and the troop here, to take care of us, as he said.

"Mr. Watts, Miss Sally, is a very worthy man; but, poor soul, he is so captivated with you,—the pain in his breast all owing to you,—he was caught by this beauty-spot," tapping my cheek. He could not have thought it was meant for an addition, as the size of it shew'd the contrary. But he is gone; and I think, as I have escap'd thus far safe, I am quite a heroine, and need not be fearful of any of the lords of the creation for the future.

Six o'clock, Even&.

Watts drank tea with us. A conversable man. Says that the Dandridges are one of the genteelest families in

Virginia,—relations of General Washington's wife. He appeared very fond of the Captain, who has had a liberal education. Very sensible and brave.

I sat in the entry all last evening, as did Betsy. But first, let me say, Fifth-day morn we chatted on a variety of subjects; and amongst others, he mentioned the cruelty of the Britons, which, I agreed, was very great. He said he wou'd retaliate whenever he had an opportunity.

I strenuously oppos'd such a procedure, observing that it would be erring in the same way, and tho' they might deserve it, yet it wou'd be much nobler to treat them with lenity. Remember those lines of Pope,—

> "That mercy I to others shew,
> That mercy shew to me."

"I perfectly remember them. Your sentiments are noble; but we must retaliate sometimes."

A horseman deliver'd this message: "Let the troop lie on their arms, and be ready to march at a moment's warning."

He immediately gave those orders to the sergeant. Every soldier was in motion. I was a good deal frighten'd, and ask'd Watts the reason. He fancy'd the British were in motion, tho' he had not receiv'd such intelligence.

"What will thee do if they come here?"

"Defend the house as long as I can, ma'am."

I was shock'd. "Bless my heart; what *will* become of us?"

"You may be very safe. The house is an excellent house to defend; only do you be still. If the British vanquish us, down on your knees, and cry, 'Bless the king.' If we conquer them, why, you know you are safe."

This added to my fright. I called my dear mamma, who was much indispos'd. Dadda was gone to Lancaster. Mamma ask'd him the same questions, and he gave her the same answers. I was in a fearful taking, and said that if I thought such a thing wou'd happen, I wou'd set off, tho' nine o'clock, and walk to Uncle Foulke's.

"No, don't go to-night, Miss Sally. I will take you there to-morrow. Don't be uneasy. This is nothing. I often go to bed with my boots on upon some alarms."

"But will thee take off thy boots to-night?"

"Yes, I will, indeed."

"Is thee really in earnest about defending the house?"

"No, madam; for believe me, if I hear the enemy is in motion, depend upon it, I will immediately depart, bag and baggage."

This dispell'd my fears, and after wishes for a good night, he retir'd to his chamber. Imagine my consternation when our girl came running in, and said that the lane was filled with light horse. I flew to the side door. It was true.

My joy was great when I heard Major Clough ask if this was Capt. Dandridge's quarters. I answered in the affirmative. He rode round to the other door. Watts, tho' gone to bed, was call'd. He chatted apart to the Major a while, then went off towards Skippack road, follow'd by a large party of horse and waggons.

My fears were all renew'd; and, as if we were to be in perpetual alarms, by came another party, much larger than the other, in dark clothes. These we all thought were British. They halted. All as still as death. The officer rode up to the door.

"Does Mr. Foulke live here?"

"Yes," said somebody.

"Is there not a family from town here,—Mr. Wister's?"

I recollected the voice, and said, "Captain Stoddard, I presume?"

"Yes, madam. Are you Mr. Wister's wife?"

"No, his daughter."

"Is your papa at home?"

"No," I reply'd, but invited him in to see mamma.

He agreed; dismounted, as did many other officers; but he alone came into our parlour. Watts follow'd, to bid us adieu. They sat a few minutes; told us that two of their men had deserted, and when that was the case, they generally mov'd their quarters. Watts told him how I was frightened. He said I paid but a poor compliment to their cavalry. I only smil'd. The alarm had partly deprived me of the power of speech.

They sat about fifteen minutes, then rose, and after the politest adieus, departed. All the horse follow'd—about one hundred and fifty. I never saw more regularity observ'd, or so undisturb'd a silence kept up when so large a number of people were together. Not a voice was heard, except that of the officer who gave the word of command.

The moon at intervals broke thro' the heavy black clouds. No noise was perceiv'd, save that which the horses made as they trotted o'er the wooden bridge across the race. Echo a while gave us back the sound. At last nothing was left but the remembrance of them. The family all retir'd to their respective chambers, and enjoyed a calm repose.

The Captain Stoddard is from New England, and belongs to Col. Sheldon's regiment of dragoons. He made an acquaintance with my father at Germantown, whilst our Army was at that place, and had been here once before. He is clever and gentlemanly.

Fifth Day, June 4th, 2 o'clock.

Oh, gracious! how warm is this day. But, warm as it is, I must make a slight alteration in my dress. I do not make an elegant figure, tho' I do not expect to see the face of a stranger to-day.

Sixth Day, June 5th, Morn, 11 o'clock.

Last night we were a little alarm'd. I was awaken'd about 12 o'clock with somebody's opening the chamber door. I observ'd Cousin Prissa talking to Mamma. I asked what was the matter.

"Only a party of light horse."

"Are they Americans?" I quickly said.

She answer'd in the affirmative (which dispell'd my fears), and told me Major Jameson commanded, and that Capts. Call and Nixon were with him. With this intelligence she left us, and I revolved in my mind whether or not Jameson would renew his acquaintance; but Morpheus buried all my ideas, and this morn I rose by or near seven, dress'd in my light chintz, which is made gown-fashion, kenting handkerchief, and linen apron.

"Sufficiently smart for a country girl, Sally."

Don't call me a country girl, Debby Norris. Please to observe that I pride myself upon being a Philadelphian, and that a residence of 20 months has not at all diminished the love I have for that dear place; and as soon as one very capital alteration takes place (which is very much talk'd of at present), I expect to return to it with a double pleasure.

Dress'd as above, down I came, and went down to our kitchen, which is a small distance from the house. As I came back I saw Jameson at the window. He met me in the entry, bow'd:—"How do you do, Miss Sally?"

After the compliments usual on such occasions had pass'd, I invited him into our parlour. He follow'd me in. We chatted very sociably.

I inquir'd for Polly Fishbourn. He said he had seen her last First-day; that she was well. Her mamma had gone to Lancaster, to visit her daughter Wharton, who, as I suppose you have heard, has lost her husband.

I ask'd him whether Dandridge was on this side the Delaware. He said "Yes." I wanted sadly to hear his opinion, but he said not a word.

The conversation turn'd upon the British leaving Philad[a]. He firmly believ'd they were going. I sincerely wish'd it might be true, but was afraid to flatter myself. I had heard it so often that I was quite faithless, and express'd my approbation of Pope's 12th beatitude, "Blessed are they that expect nothing, for they shall not be disappointed." He smil'd, and assur'd me they were going away.

He was summon'd to breakfast. I ask'd him to stay with us. He declin'd the invitation with politeness, adding that he was in a hurry,—oblig'd to go to Camp as soon as he could. He bow'd, "Your servant, ladies," and withdrew immediately. After breakfast they set off for Valley Forge, where Gen'l Washington's army still are.

I am more pleas'd with Major Jameson than I was at first. He is sensible and agreeable,—a manly person, and a very good countenance. We girls differ about him. Prissa and I admire him, whilst Liddy and Betsy will not allow him a spark of beauty. Aunt's family are charm'd with his behaviour,—so polite, so unassuming. When he disturb'd them last night, he made a hundred apologies,—was so sorry to call them up,—'twas real necessity oblig'd him.

I can't help remarking the contrast between him and Dandridge. The former appears to be rather grave than gay,—no vain, assuming airs. The latter calls for the genius of a Hogarth to characterize him. He is possess'd of a good understanding, a very liberal education, gay and volatile to excess. He is an Indian, a gentleman, grave and sad in the same hour.

But what signifies? I can't give thee a true idea of him; but he assumes at pleasure a behaviour the most courtly, the most elegant of anything I ever saw. He is very entertaining company, and very vain of his personal beauties; yet nevertheless his character is exceptional.

Sixth Day, Noon and Eveng.

Nothing material occurr'd.

Seventh Day Night.

A dull morn. In the afternoon, Liddy, Betsy, R. H. and self went to one of our neighbours to eat strawberries. Got a few. Return'd home; drank tea. No beaus. Adieu.

First Day, Even'g.

High-ho! Debby, there's no little meaning in that exclamation, ain't there. To me it conveys much. I have been looking what the dictionary says. It denotes uneasiness of mind. I don't know that my mind is particularly uneasy just now.

The occurrences of the day come now. I left my chamber between eight and nine, breakfasted, went up to dress, put on a new purple and white striped Persian, white petticoat, muslin apron, gauze cap, and handkerchief. Thus array'd, Miss Norris, I ask your opinion. Thy partiality to thy friend will bid thee say I made a tolerable appearance. Not so, my dear. I was this identical Sally Wister, with all her whims and follies; and they have gain'd so great an ascendency over my prudence, that I fear it will be a hard matter to divest myself of them. But I will hope for a reformation.

Cousin Hannah Miles came about nine, and spent the day with us. After we had din'd, two dragoons rode up to the door; one a waiting-man of Dandridge's, the faithful Jonathan. They are quarter'd a few miles from us.

The junior sisters (Liddy and Betsy), join'd by me, ventur'd to send our compliments to the Captain and Watts. Prissa insists that it is vastly indelicate, and that she has done with us. Hey day! What prudish notions are those, Priscilla! I banish prudery. Suppose we had sent our love to him, where had been the impropriety?

for really he had a person that was love-inspiring, tho'
I escap'd, and may say, *Io triumphe*. I answer not for the
other girls, but am apt to conclude that Cupid shot his
arrows, and may be they had effect.

A fine evening this. If wishes cou'd avail, I wou'd be
in your garden with S. Jones, P. Fishbourn, and thyself.
Thee has no objection to some of our North Wales
swains,—not the beaus inhabitants of N—— W——,
but some of the transitory ones. But cruel reverse. Instead of having my wishes accomplish'd I must confine
myself to the narrow limits of this farm.

Liddy calls: "Sally, will thee walk?" "Yes." Perhaps
a walk will give a new turn to my ideas, and present
something new to my vacant imagination.

Second Day, Third Day, Fourth Day.

No new occurrences to relate. Almost adventure-
less, except Gen'l Lacy's riding by, and his fierce horse
disdaining to go without shewing his airs, in expectation of drawing the attention of the Mill girls, in order
to glad his master's eyes. Ha! ha! ha! One would have
imagin'd that vanity had been buried amidst the shades
of N. Wales.

Lacy is tolerable; but as ill luck wou'd order it, I
had been busy, and my auburn ringlets were much
dishevell'd; therefore I did not glad his eyes, and cannot set down in the list of honours receiv'd that of a
bow from Brigadier-Gen'l Lacy.

Fifth Day Night, June 18th.

Rose at half-past four this morning. Iron'd industriously till one o'clock, din'd, went up stairs, threw myself on the bed, and fell asleep. About four sister Hannah waked me, and said uncle and Foulke were down stairs; so I decorated myself, and went down. Felt quite lackadaisical. However, I jump'd about a little, and the stupid fit went off.

We have had strange reports about the British being about leaving Philad[a]. I can't believe it. Adieu.

Sixth Day Morn, June 19th.

We have heard an astonishing piece of news!—that the English have entirely left the city! It is almost impossible! Stay, I shall hear further.

Sixth Day Eve.

A light horseman has just confirm'd the above intelligence! This is *charmante*! They decamp'd yesterday. He (the horseman) was in Philad[a]. It is true. They have gone. Past a doubt. I can't help forbear exclaiming to the girls,—

"Now are you sure the news is true? Now are you sure they have gone?"

"Yes, yes, yes!" they all cry, "and may they never, never return."

Dr. Gould came here to-night. Our army are about six miles off, on their march to the Jerseys.

Seventh Day Morn.

O. F. arrived just now, and relateth as *followeth:*— The Army began their march at six this morn by their house. Our worthy Gen'l Smallwood breakfasted at Uncle Caleb's. He ask'd how Mr. & Mrs. Wister and the young ladies were, and sent his respects to us.

Our brave, our heroic General Washington was escorted by fifty of the Life Guard, with drawn swords. Each day he acquires an addition to his goodness.

We have been very anxious to hear how the inhabitants have far'd. I understand that Gen'l Arnold, who bears a good character, has the command of the city, and the soldiers conducted with great decorum. Smallwood says that they had the strictest orders to behave well; and I dare say they obey'd the order. I now think of nothing but returning to Philadelphia.

So shall now conclude this journal with humbly hoping that the Great Disposer of events, who has graciously vouchsaf'd to protect us to this day through many dangers, will still be pleas'd to continue his protection.

Sally Wister
North Wales, June 20th, 1778.